NEW JERSEY

BY RACHEL GRACK

BELLWETHER MEDIA • MINNEAPOLIS, MN

Blastoff! Discovery launches a new mission: reading to learn. Filled with facts and features, each book offers you an exciting new world to explore!

BLASTOFF! UNIVERSE

BLASTOFF! Beginners — GRADE K

BLASTOFF! READERS — GRADES 1-3

BLASTOFF! DISCOVERY — GRADE 4

This edition first published in 2022 by Bellwether Media, Inc.

No part of this publication may be reproduced in whole or in part without written permission of the publisher.
For information regarding permission, write to Bellwether Media, Inc., Attention: Permissions Department,
6012 Blue Circle Drive, Minnetonka, MN 55343.

Library of Congress Cataloging-in-Publication Data

Names: Koestler-Grack, Rachel A., 1973- author.
Title: New Jersey / Rachel Grack.
Description: Minneapolis, MN : Bellwether Media, 2022. | Series: Blastoff! Discovery: State profiles | Includes bibliographical references and index. | Audience: Ages 7-13 | Audience: Grades 4-6 | Summary: "Engaging images accompany information about New Jersey. The combination of high-interest subject matter and narrative text is intended for students in grades 3 through 8"– Provided by publisher.
Identifiers: LCCN 2021020872 (print) | LCCN 2021020873 (ebook) | ISBN 9781644873359 (library binding) | ISBN 9781648341786 (ebook)
Subjects: LCSH: New Jersey–Juvenile literature.
Classification: LCC F134.3 .K64 2021 (print) | LCC F134.3 (ebook) | DDC 974.9–dc23
LC record available at https://lccn.loc.gov/2021020872
LC ebook record available at https://lccn.loc.gov/2021020873

Editor: Betsy Rathburn   Designer: Andrea Schneider

Printed in the United States of America, North Mankato, MN.

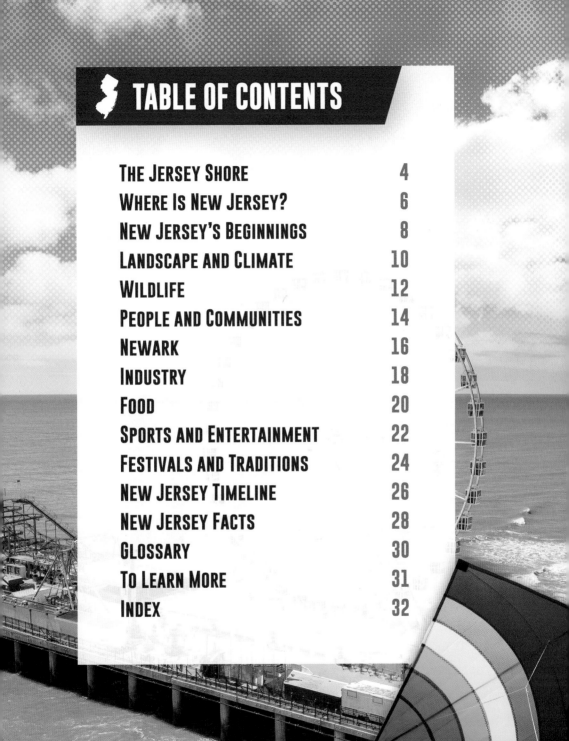

TABLE OF CONTENTS

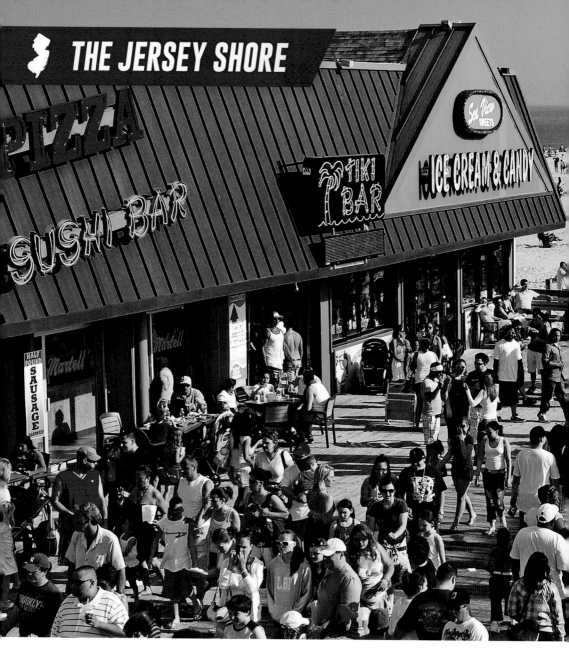

A family arrives bright and early for their day on the Jersey Shore. They carry beach bags, towels, and umbrellas onto the sand. The sun is shining, and the water is warm. It is time to swim! They run into the water, jumping over small waves.

BUTTERMILK FALLS

PALISADES INTERSTATE PARK

SANDY HOOK LIGHTHOUSE

TRIPOD ROCK

POINT PLEASANT
BOARDWALK
JERSEY SHORE

At lunchtime, they head to a restaurant along the boardwalk. Each family member enjoys a slice of pizza, followed by a cold cup of Italian ice. Later, they take a ride on the Ferris wheel. From the top, they can see the ocean stretched out for miles. Welcome to New Jersey!

New Jersey is a small state on the East Coast of the United States. It has an area of 8,723 square miles (22,592 square kilometers). It is the fourth-smallest state. New York lies to the northeast. The Hudson River separates the states along the northeastern border. The Atlantic Ocean lies to the east. The Delaware Bay is to the south. To the west, the Delaware River separates New Jersey from Pennsylvania and Delaware.

Trenton, the state capital, sits along the Delaware River in west-central New Jersey. Other important cities include Newark, Jersey City, and Paterson in the northeast.

NEW YORK

HUDSON
RIVER

PATERSON

JERSEY
CITY

NEWARK

PENNSYLVANIA

TRENTON

DELAWARE
RIVER

NEW JERSEY

DELAWARE
BAY

DELAWARE

ATLANTIC
OCEAN

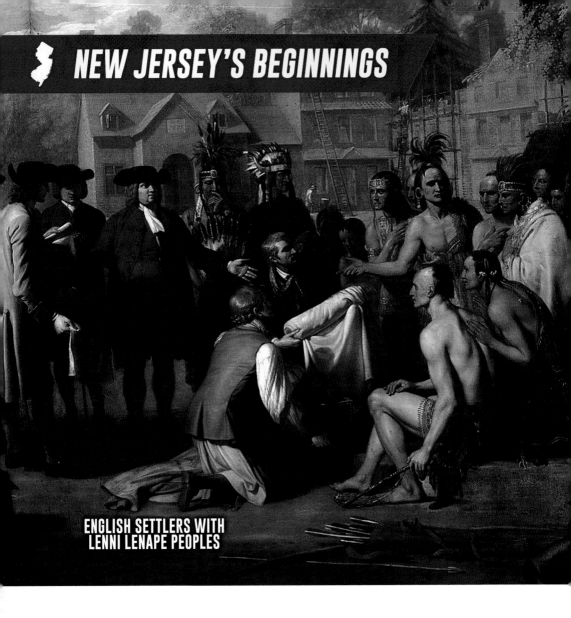

NEW JERSEY'S BEGINNINGS

ENGLISH SETTLERS WITH
LENNI LENAPE PEOPLES

People first arrived in New Jersey more than 10,000 years ago. Over time, Native American tribes formed. The Lenni Lenape were the most prominent. In 1524, Italian explorer Giovanni da Verrazzano visited the area. **Settlers** from England and the Netherlands soon followed. Bergen became the first permanent European settlement in 1660. Four years later, New Jersey became one of the 13 original **colonies**.

New Jersey played an important role during the **Revolutionary War**. Over 100 battles took place there! In 1787, New Jersey became the third state to join the United States.

REVOLUTIONARY WAR

NATIVE PEOPLES OF NEW JERSEY

RAMAPOUGH LENAPE

- Original lands covered northeastern United States
- Around 5,000 members today

POWHATAN RENAPE

- Original lands covered northeastern United States
- Less than 1,000 members today

NANTICOKE LENNI-LENAPE

- Original lands covered all of New Jersey, northern Delaware, eastern Pennsylvania, and southeastern New York
- Around 3,000 members today

The Atlantic Coastal **Plain** covers southern New Jersey. Within it is a vast area of trees called the Pine Barrens. The rolling hills of the Piedmont spread across north-central New Jersey. The rocky Highlands lie just to the north. The rugged Ridge and Valley cuts through the northwest corner of the state. On the coast, **lagoons** separate **barrier islands** from the rest of the state.

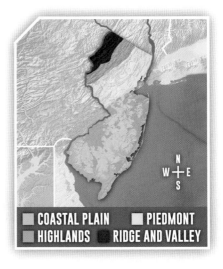

COASTAL PLAIN   PIEDMONT
HIGHLANDS   RIDGE AND VALLEY

HIGHLANDS
ABRAM S. HEWITT STATE FOREST

PINE BARRENS

SPRING
HIGH: 61°F (16°C)
LOW: 42°F (6°C)

SUMMER
HIGH: 83°F (28°C)
LOW: 65°F (18°C)

FALL
HIGH: 66°F (19°C)
LOW: 47°F (8°C)

WINTER
HIGH: 43°F (6°C)
LOW: 26°F (-3°C)

°F = degrees Fahrenheit
°C = degrees Celsius

Winters are cold through most of New Jersey. Heavy snowstorms are common in the northwest. Summers get **humid** and hot. Thunderstorms are common. In the summer and fall, **hurricanes** may hit the coast.

RED-TAILED HAWK

New Jersey is home to many animal species. In the Highlands, hawks and eagles swoop on snakes and lizards. Black bears, white-tailed deer, and bobcats roam the Ridge and Valley. Across the Piedmont, woodpeckers knock on trees while falcons hunt woodrats and salamanders.

BOBCAT

Rare bog turtles are New Jersey's state reptile. They live in wetlands across the state. Colorful Pine Barrens tree frogs are found only in southern New Jersey! Along the Atlantic coast, herons wade through wetlands, jabbing at fish, frogs, and reptiles. Whales, dolphins, and sea turtles can be spotted from shore.

PINE BARRENS TREE FROG

HUMPBACK WHALE

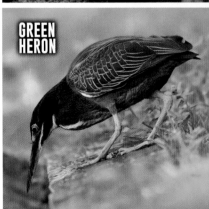

GREEN HERON

NEW JERSEY'S FUTURE: ANIMAL HABITATS

New Jersey's growing population puts wildlife in danger. Forests and fields are cleared as cities expand. Lakes and rivers get polluted. This destroys animal habitats. Species may face extinction if their homes are not protected.

BOG TURTLE

Life Span: up to 50 years
Status: critically endangered

bog turtle range =

LEAST CONCERN	NEAR THREATENED	VULNERABLE	ENDANGERED	CRITICALLY ENDANGERED	EXTINCT IN THE WILD	EXTINCT

13

More than 9 million people live in New Jersey. Its small size and big population give the state the highest **population density** in the United States. About 9 out of 10 New Jerseyans live in **urban** areas. Many live in large cities such as Newark or Jersey City. Members of the state's small Native American population may live on **reservations**.

ATLANTIC CITY

More than half of New Jerseyans have European **ancestors**. Hispanic residents make up the next-largest group, followed by Black or African Americans and Asian Americans. In recent years, **immigrants** have come to New Jersey. Newcomers are from India, the Dominican Republic, and Mexico.

NEWARK

PASSAIC RIVER

In 1666, colonists founded the town that would become Newark. It grew into a busy shipping center because of its location on the Passaic River and Newark Bay. By the 1800s, Newark was known for leather, jewelry, and shoe **manufacturing**.

ALL ABOARD!

Newark is a short train ride from New York City. Many people travel between the two cities for work. This brings a lot of business to both cities.

Today, Newark is New Jersey's largest city. It is a major shipping center. Businesses still make leather goods and jewelry. Electronics, furniture, and publishing are also big industries. People in Newark gather at the Prudential Center for concerts and events. They browse art at the Newark Museum. Branch Brook Park is popular when its cherry blossom trees bloom in spring!

BRANCH BROOK PARK

HARVESTING CRANBERRIES

NEW JERSEY'S FUTURE: CLEAN ENERGY

New Jersey set a goal to use only clean energy by 2050. Manufacturers face challenges meeting this goal. It can cost a lot of money. Some businesses may find success with solar and wind energy.

New Jersey was a top supplier of iron ore in the 1800s. Today, granite, sand, and gravel are mined instead. Fishing and timber are also important **natural resources**. New Jersey has good farming soil, too. It is a leading producer of blueberries, cranberries, and eggplant. Other major crops include peaches, asparagus, and bell peppers.

Most New Jerseyans work **service jobs** at schools, hospitals, or stores. Many others work in manufacturing. They make medicine, medical equipment, and electronics. Chemicals and processed foods are also made in New Jersey.

INVENTED IN NEW JERSEY

CAMPBELL'S SOUP

Date Invented: 1869

Inventor: Joseph A. Campbell

PHONOGRAPH

Date Invented: 1877

Inventor: Thomas Edison

ELECTRIC LIGHT BULB

Date Invented: 1879

Inventor: Thomas Edison

DRIVE-IN THEATERS

Date Invented: 1933

Inventors: Richard Hollingshead, Park-In Theaters

PORK ROLL

New Jersey has many tasty dishes. Italian hot dogs are served inside a pizza crust and topped with peppers, potatoes, and onions. Tomato pies are also inspired by Italy. They are like upside-down pizzas. There is cheese on the crust and tomato on top!

ITALIAN HOT DOG

TOMATO PIE

Pork rolls are another state favorite. Ground ham is sliced, fried, and stacked in an egg sandwich. A New Jersey-style sloppy joe is a deli meat sandwich topped with Swiss cheese, coleslaw, and Russian dressing. Lobster, fish, and crab sandwiches are popular along the Jersey Shore. Salt water taffy is a favorite sweet.

SALT WATER TAFFY

35 SERVINGS

Have an adult help you make this recipe.

INGREDIENTS

1 cup granulated sugar

2/3 cup light corn syrup

1/2 cup water

1 tablespoon unsalted butter

1 tablespoon cornstarch

1 teaspoon salt

1/2 teaspoon flavor extract

food coloring

DIRECTIONS

1. Grease one 8-inch baking pan.

2. In a 2-quart saucepan over medium heat, combine all ingredients except flavor and color. Mix well and bring to a boil.

3. Heat without stirring until candy thermometer reads 255 degrees Fahrenheit (124 degrees Celsius).

4. Remove from heat. Stir in flavor and color, if desired. Pour into baking pan.

5. Let stand until cool enough to handle.

6. Lightly grease hands. Form a big ball, then fold, double, and pull the taffy until it is light in color and stiff.

7. Roll into a long rope. Then, cut taffy into pieces with greased scissors. Wrap pieces with wax paper.

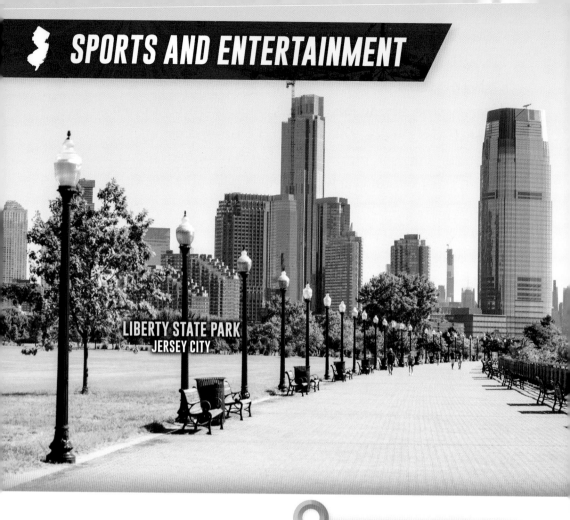

LIBERTY STATE PARK
JERSEY CITY

Football is one of New Jersey's most popular sports. The New York Jets and New York Giants both play in New Jersey. Hockey fans root for the New Jersey Devils or the Metropolitan Riveters. Many people cheer for the NJ/NY Gotham FC soccer team, too.

ARCADE FUN

Asbury Park, New Jersey, is home to a pinball museum! The Silverball Pinball Museum has dozens of pinball machines from past decades.

There are many places to see art in New Jersey. People wander the sculpture park at the Grounds for Sculpture in Hamilton. The Princeton University Art Museum displays over 80,000 art pieces. Boardwalks along the Jersey Shore draw many visitors in the summertime. State park hiking is also popular. Winter draws people outside for skiing and snowboarding.

GROUNDS FOR SCULPTURE

NOTABLE SPORTS TEAM

New Jersey Devils
Sport: National Hockey League
Started: 1982
Place of Play: Prudential Center

FESTIVALS AND TRADITIONS

New Jerseyans celebrate the many **cultures** that shape their state! Each June, thousands of people visit the Hungarian Festival in New Brunswick. They eat **traditional** foods and watch folk dances. In August, the Puerto Rican **Heritage** Festival and Parade travels the streets of Jersey City. The Hoboken Italian Festival draws crowds every September. People cheer on competitors in the pizza eating contest!

HUNGARIAN
FESTIVAL
NEW BRUNSWICK

WILDWOODS INTERNATIONAL KITE FESTIVAL
JERSEY SHORE

WINTER IN THE PINES

Every year, Winter in the Pines draws people to the historic village of Batsto in central New Jersey. People take old-fashioned carriage rides, listen to music, and explore New Jersey history!

The Jersey Shore hosts celebrations, too. Each May, the sky fills with colorful kites at the Wildwoods International Kite Festival. In July, people look out for decorated boats at Ocean City's Night in Venice boat parade. There is always something to celebrate in New Jersey!

NEW JERSEY TIMELINE

1524

Giovanni da Verrazzano is the first known European to explore New Jersey

1664

New Jersey becomes an English colony

1776 TO 1783

New Jersey is an important battleground of the Revolutionary War

1660

Bergen, later renamed Jersey City, becomes the first permanent European settlement in New Jersey

1666

Colonists found present-day Newark

1787

New Jersey becomes the 3rd state

1861 TO 1865

New Jerseyans fight for the Union Army during the Civil War

2012

Hurricane Sandy hits New Jersey, causing massive damage

1993

Christine Todd Whitman is elected New Jersey's first female governor

1978

The Pinelands becomes the first U.S. national reserve

2020

Fabiana Pierre-Louis becomes the first Black woman to join New Jersey's state supreme court

1995

The New Jersey Devils hockey team wins the Stanley Cup for the first time

Nickname: The Garden State

Motto: Liberty and Prosperity

Date of Statehood: December 18, 1787 (the 3rd state)

Capital City: Trenton ★

Other Major Cities: Newark, Jersey City, Paterson

Area: 8,723 square miles (22,592 square kilometers); New Jersey is the 4th smallest state.

Population

9,288,994
(2020)

STATE FLAG

New Jersey's state flag is light yellow. In its center is the state steal. A blue shield has three plows in it. These represent New Jersey's farming. On top of the shield is a helmet. Above the helmet is a horse, New Jersey's state animal. Two Roman goddesses, Libertas and Ceres, stand on either side of the shield. They represent the state motto. A blue banner below the shield shows the state motto and the year the seal was adopted.

INDUSTRY

Main Exports

chemicals   medical drugs   electronics

plants   fruit

MANUFACTURING
5%

FARMING AND NATURAL RESOURCES
4%

GOVERNMENT
11%

SERVICES
80%

JOBS

Natural Resources
stone, sand, gravel, fish, timber

GOVERNMENT

14 ELECTORAL VOTES

Federal Government

12 | 2
REPRESENTATIVES | SENATORS

USA

NJ

State Government

80 | 40
REPRESENTATIVES | SENATORS

STATE SYMBOLS

STATE BIRD
EASTERN GOLDFINCH

STATE ANIMAL
HORSE

STATE FLOWER
COMMON BLUE VIOLET

STATE TREE
NORTHERN RED OAK

GLOSSARY

ancestors—relatives who lived long ago

barrier islands—long, sandy islands along a shore created by wind and waves

colonies—distant territories which are under the control of another nation

cultures—beliefs, arts, and ways of life in places or societies

heritage—the traditions, achievements, and beliefs that are part of the history of a group of people

humid—having a lot of moisture in the air

hurricanes—storms formed in the tropics that have violent winds and often have rain and lightning

immigrants—people who move to a new country

lagoons—shallow bodies of water that connect to a larger body of water

manufacturing—a field of work in which people use machines to make products

natural resources—materials in the earth that are taken out and used to make products or fuel

plain—a large area of flat land

population density—a measure of how crowded a place is based on the number of people per square mile

reservations—areas of land that are controlled by Native American tribes

Revolutionary War—a war for independence from Britain fought from 1775 to 1783

service jobs—jobs that perform tasks for people or businesses

settlers—people who move to live in a new, undeveloped region

traditional—related to customs, ideas, or beliefs handed down from one generation to the next

urban—related to cities and city life

AT THE LIBRARY

Murray, Julie. *New Jersey*. Minneapolis, Minn.: Abdo Publishing, 2020.

Stanley, Joseph. *Delaware (Lenape)*. New York, N.Y.: PowerKids Press, 2016.

Yomtov, Nel. *New Jersey*. New York, N.Y.: Children's Press, 2018.

ON THE WEB

FACTSURFER

Factsurfer.com gives you a safe, fun way to find more information.

1. Go to www.factsurfer.com.

2. Enter "New Jersey" into the search box and click Q.

3. Select your book cover to see a list of related content.

INDEX